EXPLORATION

Peggy J. Parks

BLACKBIRCH PRESS

An imprint of Thomson Gale, a part of The Thomson Corporation

Detroit • New York • San Francisco • San Diego • New Haven, Conn. • Waterville, Maine • London • Munich

Picture Credits

Cover: © Property of Blackbirch Press (top); NASA (bottom)
© AFP/Getty Images, 23 (top), 30 (bottom)
© Yann Arthus-Bertrand/CORBIS, 6
© David Ball/CORBIS, 20
© Bettmann/CORBIS, 5 (bottom), 13 (bottom), 17 (top), 21 (bottom), 23 (bottom)
© Stefano Bianchetti/CORBIS, 15 (bottom), 16 (top)
© CORBIS, 24 (left)
Corel Corporation, 7 (bottom left), 15 (top), 26 (bottom), 31
© Graeme Cornwallis/Lonely Planet Images, 8 (bottom)
© Lowell Georgia/CORBIS, 18
© Tria Giovan/CORBIS, 19 (bottom)
© Hulton Archive by Getty Images, 10 (top), 19 (top), 24 (right)
Library and Archives Canada, 9
NASA, 26 (top), 27 (top and bottom), 28 (bottom) and middle), 29
National Geographic Society, 4
© Alan Nogues/CORBIS, 13 (top)
North Wind Picture Archives, 5 (top), 6 (top), 10 (bottom), 11, 12, 14 (top and bottom), 16 (bottom), 17 (bottom)
© Photos.com, 25 (top), 28 (top), 30 (top)
© Royalty-Free/CORBIS, 8 (top)
© Ralph White/CORBIS, 22
© Staffan Widstrand/CORBIS, 21 (top)
© Sandro Vannini/CORBIS, 7 (insets)

LIBRARY OF CONGRESS CATALOGING-IN-PUBLICATION DATA

Parks, Peggy J., 1951–
  Exploration / by Peggy J. Parks.
      p. cm. — (Yesterday & today)
  Includes bibliographical references.
  ISBN 1-56711-831-3 (hardcover : alk. paper)
  1. Discoveries in geography—Juvenile literature. I. Title. II. Series: Yesterday and Today.

  G175.P3378 2005
  910'.9—dc22   2004022110

Table of Contents

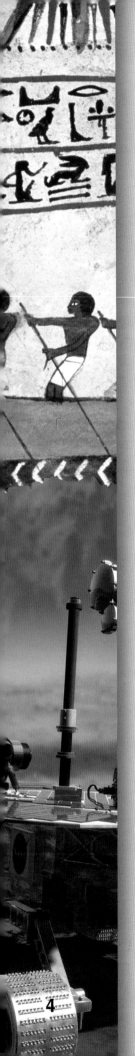

The First Explorers

People who lived hundreds of thousands of years ago were certainly curious about the world around them, and they had the desire to explore it. Unlike modern explorers, however, it is unlikely that these ancient humans explored in search of adventure. Instead, they probably explored because their lives depended on it. They needed places to live where the climate was favorable and fresh water and food were plentiful.

The first humans to make records of their exploration were the Egyptians. In about 3500 B.C., they made many journeys up and down the Nile River. Their goal was to find people from other areas with whom they could trade goods. Timber was scarce in the Nile valley, so they built boats with bundles of papyrus, a stalky aquatic

A wall painting shows early Egyptians traveling down the Nile River.

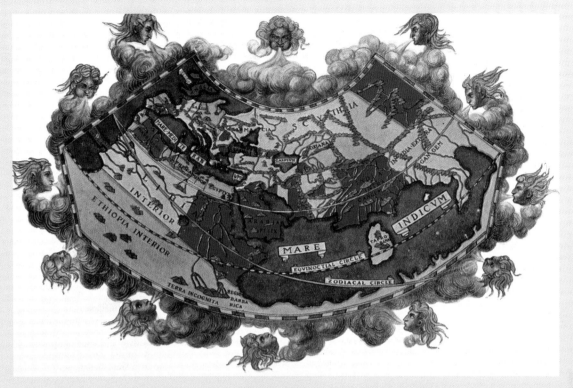

Some ancient people believed Earth was flat and oblong, as illustrated by this 2nd-century map.

Prehistory —

500 B.C. —

100 B.C. —

A.D. 100 —

200 —

500 —

1000 —

1200 —

1300 —

1400 —

1500 —

1600 —

1700 —

1800 —

1900 —

2000 —

2100 —

plant that grew along the riverbanks. The boats were powered by men using oars, as well as by small square sails.

The Nile flowed from south to north. The Egyptians could row downstream with the current and then sail upstream with the wind. Their earliest journeys were limited to the river because their papyrus boats were too fragile to withstand rough ocean waters. Also, these early explorers did not have tools to help with navigation. They had to rely on their instincts and what they could see, hear, smell, and touch.

Modern explorers use drawings to re-create an ancient Egyptian boat out of papyrus.

Although ancient humans had no navigational tools, they found ways to explore the world around them. In boats made of papyrus, they traveled the Nile River in search of places to live, food to eat, and people with whom they could trade.

5

The Egyptians traded with the Phoenicians for cedar (below) to build ships like this Phoenician galley (above).

Seaworthy Boats

The Egyptians wanted to explore other areas beyond the Nile River, but their papyrus boats were not seaworthy. The only way they could travel on the ocean was to build wooden boats that could withstand the pounding waves. So, they decided to search for sources of timber.

Beginning about 2600 B.C., the Egyptians sailed up the Nile until they reached the Mediterranean Sea. Staying close to the coastline, they traveled to the region that is now Lebanon. There they found the Phoenicians, ancient peoples who lived along the Mediterranean's shores. The Egyptians provided raw materials to the Phoenicians in exchange for cedar. Afterward, they returned to their villages and used the wood to build boats.

In around 2500 B.C., a fleet of Egyptian ships set sail on the Red Sea. Their mission was to search for a legendary "Land of the Gods" known as Punt. They believed it was the home of their earliest ancestors. They had also heard about valuable treasures in the mysterious land, such as ebony, ivory, silver, gold, and incense to burn on their altars. Their voyage to Punt was successful. When the fleet returned to Egypt, the ships were filled with valuable cargo. In search of more riches, they made several voyages to Punt between 2000 and 1493 B.C.

Historians are not sure exactly where Punt was located, but they believe it was somewhere in southern Africa. If that was the case, the Egyptians traveled the full length of the Red Sea and on into the Indian Ocean. During the journey, they would have covered more than 8,000 miles (12,875km). That was an amazing feat of exploration that would have been impossible without sturdy wooden boats.

Prehistory

500 B.C.

100 B.C.

A.D. 100

200

500

1000

1200

1300

1400

1500

1600

1700

1800

1900

2000

2100

Ancient Navigational Technique

Early explorers who traveled the ocean did not have compasses or other navigational tools. Instead, they stayed near the shoreline and paid close attention to landmarks. By memorizing where the landmarks were, they could find their way back home.

The early Egyptians traveled many miles to Punt in search of riches such as gold (above) and ivory (left).

The Calibrated Sundial

Like the Egyptians, the Greeks were also adventurers as well as expert navigators. One Greek explorer, Pytheas, invented an instrument called the calibrated sundial. This tool was extremely valuable because it allowed him to accurately determine latitude, or his position north or south of the equator. Around 330 B.C., Pytheas set sail from his hometown of Massalia, a Greek colony in France. He used the

The Greek explorer Pytheas invented the calibrated sundial (above) to determine latitude. His explorations ended when he reached the icy northern seas.

The First Speedometers

To accurately chart their courses, ancient explorers needed to know how fast their ships traveled. They used an apparatus called a chip log—a long piece of rope with knots tied at equal distances apart. A piece of wood was fastened at the end, and the rope was wound on a spool. Sailors tossed the wood into the sea. As the rope unwound, they counted the knots. By using an hourglass to time their count, they could measure how fast they were moving. Today the word *knot* is still the official term for measuring speed on the water.

sundial to calculate Massalia's latitude, and then he continued to make such calculations along the way. His journey took him along the coast of France to the English Channel. He then traveled around Great Britain and up the coastline of the North Atlantic. As he got closer to the frigid Arctic region, he reached an area where no explorer had gone before: a mysterious island that was likely Iceland. Pytheas's journey ended there because he encountered what he called "frozen jellyfish seas"—a mixture of slushy ice and seawater on the ocean's surface. His ship could not pass through the frozen area, so he turned around and headed home.

Pytheas later wrote about his exploration in a book called *On the Ocean and Description of the Earth*. He told of the jellyfish seas and how the Sun shone twenty hours a day in the North Atlantic area. He also wrote about ocean tides. Tides in the Mediterranean were too small to be noticeable, so Pytheas was the first Greek to observe them. During his travels he correctly determined that tides are caused by the phases of the Moon.

Pytheas's observations were so astounding that many years passed before anyone believed him. Yet because of his vast knowledge of the sea, and his calibrated sundial, he was able to venture into faraway lands that were unknown and unexplored.

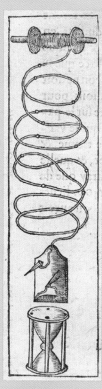

Ancient explorers used chip logs like the one in this illustration to determine how fast their ships traveled.

Prehistory ——

500 B.C. ——

100 B.C. ——

A.D. 100 ——

200 ——

500 ——

1000 ——

1200 ——

1300 ——

1400 ——

1500 ——

1600 ——

1700 ——

1800 ——

1900 ——

2000 ——

2100 ——

Viking Longships

The Vikings' longships (top) allowed them to sail across the Atlantic. Viking explorer Leif Eriksson (above) became the first European to step on North American soil.

Centuries passed before any explorer traveled as far north as Pytheas. In the late eighth century A.D., the Vikings began their own journeys through the North Atlantic. Unlike Pytheas, however, they were not just visitors to the frigid north; it was their home. Expert seamen and navigators, the Vikings lived along the Baltic Sea and the coastline of Scandinavia.

The Vikings were also known for their master shipbuilding skills. They built huge boats known as longships, which were bigger, faster, and more maneuverable than any ships ever built. One of the biggest was 119 feet (36.3m) long. It had more than seventy oars and a massive sail that measured more than 2,000 square feet (185.8 sq m). Longships enabled the Vikings to sail through ocean waters with the wind, or speed into coastal areas using teams of oarsmen. These superb ships, along with the Vikings' excellent navigational skills, allowed them to be the first explorers to sail all the way across the treacherous waters of the Atlantic Ocean.

Throughout the ninth and tenth centuries, the Vikings explored and conquered many lands. In 985, a Viking captain was headed toward Greenland when his ship was blown off course. Without realizing where he was, he ended up in North America. He continued sailing until he finally reached Greenland, where he told his fellow countrymen about the land he had accidentally discovered. Fifteen years later, a Viking explorer named Leif Eriksson made his own journey to the "New World." He became the first European to set foot on North American soil when he discovered the area that is now called Newfoundland.

For three hundred years, the Vikings crossed the Atlantic and settled new colonies. Their knowledge of the sea helped them find their way, and their superb longships carried them where they wanted to go.

Flying Navigational Tools

During the summer in high latitudes, months passed when no stars were visible in the sky. Therefore, the Vikings found other ways to navigate, such as bird-watching. If the birds' beaks were full, they were likely flying toward their nests on land. Empty beaks meant they were heading out to sea. One Viking sailor brought ravens along on his journeys. He deliberately starved the birds, and when he thought land might be near he released them. They headed toward land in search of food, and he followed—hence, the expression "as the crow flies."

Prehistory ——

500 B.C. ——

100 B.C. ——

A.D. 100 ——

200 ——

500 ——

1000 ——

1200 ——

1300 ——

1400 ——

1500 ——

1600 ——

1700 ——

1800 ——

1900 ——

2000 ——

2100 ——

The Compass

The Europeans perfected China's magnetic compass for use in their own explorations.

Like the Vikings, Chinese explorers also built sophisticated, seaworthy ships. They had a tool the Vikings did not have, however: the magnetic compass. The Chinese had studied magnetism since the third century A.D. They found that a mineral called magnetite, also called lodestone, aligned itself in a north-south direction. Early compasses were made by laying pieces of magnetite on reeds and then floating the reeds in water. Later, the Chinese learned that when they rubbed pieces of magnetite against iron or steel needles, the needles became magnetized. They used this knowledge to make compasses that could be used as navigational devices.

By the eleventh century, compasses were widely used as navigational tools on Chinese ships. During the early to mid-1400s, a Chinese admiral named Cheng Ho sailed with a massive fleet of ships to distant lands. In a series of voyages, these "Treasure Fleets" covered thousands of miles and visited nearly forty countries.

Explorers in Europe had heard about the magnetic compass, but they did not begin using it until long after it was invented by the Chinese. In 1492 an Italian explorer named Christopher Columbus used the instrument to guide the voyage of his three ships: the *Niña*, *Pinta*, and *Santa Maria*. He sailed west from

Spooky Tool

When Europeans first heard of the compass, many were suspicious of it. Some even believed its magnetic powers were a sign of black magic and a product of the Devil.

12

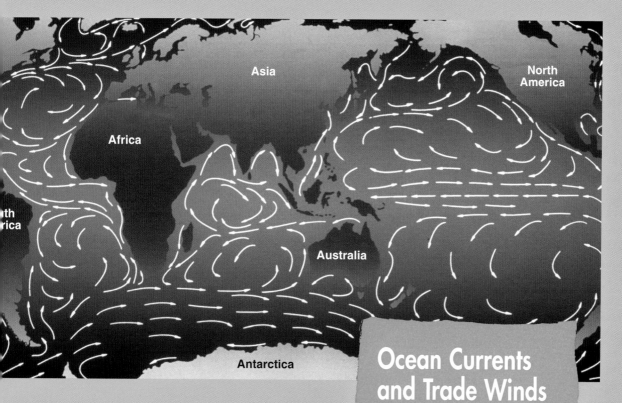

Asia

North
America

Africa

th
rica

Australia

Antarctica

Prehistory —

500 B.C. —

100 B.C. —

A.D. 100 —

200 —

500 —

1000 —

1200 —

1300 —

1400 —

1500 —

1600 —

1700 —

1800 —

1900 —

2000 —

2100 —

Europe with the goal of reaching the great landmass of Asia and its fabled cities. Instead, he reached the Caribbean Islands. Over the next ten years, Columbus made three more journeys to the land he still believed was Asia. Each time, he relied on the compass to lead him back there. In one of the trips, he discovered South America. His exploration had a major influence on the world, because it opened the door for European colonization—and the compass made it all possible.

Ocean Currents and Trade Winds

Even with navigational tools, early explorers still needed to be able to "read" natural forces. They found that ocean currents acted like powerful underwater conveyor belts that always traveled in predictable paths. Similarly, they observed that trade winds always blew in the same direction. Even when the skies were cloudy or dark, explorers could rely on these natural forces to guide them.

Christopher Columbus used a magnetic compass to guide the Niña, Pinta, *and* Santa Maria.

Cartography is both an art and a science. It involves gathering information about a geographical area and then presenting it graphically in the form of a map. The people who make maps are called cartographers. Unlike mapmakers of ancient times, modern cartographers use advanced technology to help them do their jobs. For instance, they use computer programs called geographic information systems that collect, store, and retrieve geographic data. Also, today's high-tech printing presses can produce detailed and highly accurate color maps.

The Printing Press

Another item Columbus carried along on his voyage was a copy of a journal written by explorer Marco Polo. In the journal, Polo had kept detailed notes about his exploration of Asia. Since Columbus thought he too had reached the Asian continent, he used Polo's travel log as a reference. This document was available to Columbus because of a new machine called the printing press, which played a crucial role in exploration. The machine was developed in the 1450s

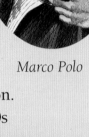

Marco Polo

Johann Gutenberg studies a map produced on his printing press. His press played a crucial role in exploration.

by a German inventor named Johann Gutenberg. For the first time, records of discovery could be printed and shared among explorers. With each new journal that was published, people became more educated about the world. This made their journeys easier, as well as much safer.

Gutenberg's invention also greatly improved cartography, or mapmaking. Before the printing press, maps were drawn by hand. It was a tedious and time-consuming job, so maps were rare and expensive. They were also unreliable, because as the maps were copied again and again, many errors were made. The printing press allowed them to be printed quickly, cheaply, and consistently, so they were much more accurate.

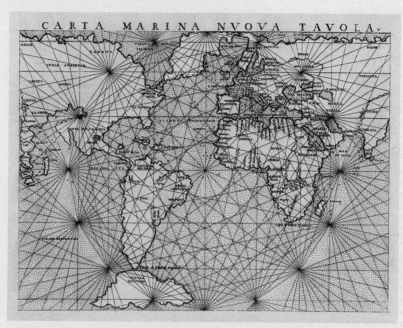

Gutenberg's printing press greatly improved mapmaking. Printed maps had fewer errors and were easy to reproduce.

One explorer who made especially good use of the printing press was Amerigo Vespucci. He had read Columbus's writings about the New World, and he made his own journey there in 1504. After his trip, Vespucci drew detailed maps and wrote elaborate reports about his discoveries. His travel documents were printed and distributed to many more people than Columbus's had been. Vespucci became so well known through his writing that a European mapping society later named the North and South American continents after him.

Although the printing press was used on land instead of on ships, it was a valuable exploration tool. It provided explorers with accurate maps and allowed them to benefit from each other's knowledge and discoveries.

Amerigo Vespucci

Prehistory ——

500 B.C. ——

100 B.C. ——

A.D. 100 ——

200 ——

500 ——

1000 ——

1200 ——

1300 ——

1400 ——

1500 ——

1600 ——

1700 ——

1800 ——

1900 ——

2000 ——

2100 ——

15

The Astrolabe and Quadrant

Ferdinand Magellan (above) relied on printed documents when he sailed in search of Asia. He used a quadrant (right) to measure latitude at night.

Another explorer who relied on printed travel documents was Ferdinand Magellan. In 1519, he set out for the New World that Columbus and Vespucci had written about. Magellan's goal was to accomplish what Columbus had been unable to do: reach Asia by sailing west from Europe. He found that it was possible to reach the Asian continent in this way. To do it, however, he had to circle the entire globe.

The compass guided Magellan in the right direction, but it did not measure latitude. For that, he relied on other navigational instruments such as the astrolabe. The astrolabe was a hand-held disk that had degrees marked around the edges and a rotating arm with small holes at each end. A navigator moved the arm until sunlight passed through the top hole and fell on the bottom hole. By checking the arm's position, the navigator could measure latitude.

At night, latitude was measured with the quadrant. This instrument was shaped like a quarter circle, with degrees marked around its curved edge. The straight edges had tiny holes on each end, and a long weighted string hung from the top. Navigators held the quadrant and lined up the holes with the North Star. Wherever the string, or plumb line, fell indicated the number of degrees latitude.

During Magellan's journey, he became the first explorer to cross the vast Pacific Ocean, and he made many discoveries. After he was killed in the Philippines in 1521, his crew continued on without him. They completed the voyage back to Spain and became the first explorers to sail around the world.

Magellan and his fellow explorers used navigational instruments that were highly advanced for the time. Because of such instruments, the explorers traveled an amazing distance and accomplished what no one had ever done before.

During daylight hours, Magellan measured latitude with an astrolabe like the one above.

The Cross-Staff

In the late sixteenth century, explorers began measuring latitude with cross-staffs, which could be used during the day or at night.

Cross-staffs were made of a wooden pole fitted with a sliding crossbar. A navigator held the instrument to his eye and pulled the slider until the Sun (or North Star) and horizon were aligned. By reading a degree scale on the cross-staff, the navigator could measure the ship's latitude.

Prehistory —

500 B.C. —

100 B.C. —

A.D. 100 —

200 —

500 —

1000 —

1200 —

1300 —

1400 —

1500 —

1600 —

1700 —

1800 —

1900 —

2000 —

2100 —

New Navigational Tools

By the eighteenth century, new instruments were available for navigation. One was the sextant, an improved device for measuring latitude. Astrolabes were often difficult to control when ships rocked in the waves. Sextants, which were similar to quadrants, used mirrors and prisms to reflect light. They were designed to allow navigators to determine their precise latitude, even from a swaying deck.

One explorer who relied on such instruments was an English captain named James Cook. Between 1766 and 1779, Cook made three voyages around the world. His goal was to find the massive southern continent known as Terra Australis Incognita, which was thought to stretch northward from the South Pole. Cook found that no such continent existed, but he did sail close enough to Antarctica to spot

The Great Barrier Reef

As good as Captain Cook's navigational instruments were, they could not detect the presence of an immense chain of reefs that stretched for thousands of miles. On his first voyage, Cook discovered Australia. But because the Great Barrier Reef was submerged underwater, he did not know it was there. He crashed into it, and his ship was nearly torn apart. Even after repairs were made, Cook and his crew were trapped in the reef for weeks. Finally the winds picked up, and they were able to sail out.

A man uses a sextant to measure latitude. The sextant's design allowed navigators to measure latitude even from a swaying ship deck.

Prehistory ⎯

500 B.C. ⎯

100 B.C. ⎯

A.D. 100 ⎯

200 ⎯

500 ⎯

1000 ⎯

1200 ⎯

1300 ⎯

1400 ⎯

1500 ⎯

1600 ⎯

1700 ⎯

1800 ⎯

1900 ⎯

2000 ⎯

2100 ⎯

icebergs. During his journey he discovered lands that had been unknown, such as New Zealand and Australia. He also explored Hawaii and many South Pacific islands.

On one of Cook's later voyages, he used an instrument called the chronometer. It was a precise timekeeping device that could determine a ship's longitude, or its distance east or west on Earth's surface. Before the chronometer, navigators had to guess at longitude by making a series of complex calculations. This was not only time-consuming, it was also often inaccurate. Miscalculations resulted in hundreds of shipwrecks. The chronometer helped Cook on his long journeys around the world. By the time he died in 1779, he had explored and charted more of the planet than any other human being.

As navigational instruments continued to be improved, they helped guide explorers through uncharted waters and into new territories. These advances in exploration helped pave the way for future adventurers to make their own journeys into the unknown.

Captain James Cook (above) used navigational tools to guide his ship on three trips around the world. He used a chronometer like this one below to find his ship's longitude.

Exploring the Ends of Earth

A modern bombarding vessel moves through thick Arctic waters. Sir William Edward Parry made three expeditions to the Arctic in the early 1800s.

Polars Firsts

In 1909, an American explorer named Robert Peary became the first person to reach the North Pole. He traveled through the frozen land in wooden sledges pulled by teams of dogs. Two years later, Norwegian explorer Roald Amundsen became the first explorer to reach the South Pole. Many explorers have followed in their footsteps, traveling by dogsled, on foot, and on snowmobiles.

Cook's exploration had taken him near Antarctica, and, centuries before, Pytheas had gotten close to the Arctic. No one had actually reached the ends of Earth, however. By the nineteenth century, the North and South poles were the only regions in the world yet to be explored. Getting to them seemed an impossible challenge because of the frozen seas.

Between 1818 and 1827, English explorer Sir William Edward Parry made three expeditions to the Arctic. He and his crew traveled as far as possible by ship and then used a technique known as sledging. Sledging was developed by the Eskimos of the Arctic and involved amphibious crafts—boats that sailed on water and were pulled by reindeer on land. Sledging helped Parry and his team travel farther north than anyone had ever

A team of dogs pull a sledge through the snow.

Prehistory ——

500 B.C. ——

100 B.C. ——

A.D. 100 ——

200 ——

500 ——

1000 ——

1200 ——

1300 ——

1400 ——

1500 ——

1600 ——

1700 ——

1800 ——

1900 ——

2000 ——

2100 ——

gone before. Still, the explorers were not able to reach the North Pole.

Exploration of Antarctica began much later than that of the Arctic. Until the mid–nineteenth century, no one knew for sure if a southernmost continent even existed. Then beginning in 1839, a man named James Ross led three expeditions to Antarctica. Ross's ship was known as a bombarding vessel, with hulls specially built to plow through thick ice. His last voyage was in 1843. While he did not succeed in reaching the bottom of the Earth, he confirmed that there was in fact a continent there.

The men who traveled to Earth's polar regions faced the greatest challenges and endured the harshest conditions of any explorers before them. With their special equipment, and their willingness to face the unknown, they became the first humans to explore the ends of Earth.

American explorer Robert Peary (below) used dog sledges to reach the North Pole in 1909.

21

The Bathysphere

Explorers were interested in the polar regions because so much about them was unknown. Yet one part of the Earth was even more mysterious: the ocean. Until the twentieth century, no one had ever explored its depths because of the dangers. At just a few hundred feet down, the water's immense weight could knock divers unconscious, or even crush them to death. Then a submersible vessel called the bathysphere was invented. It enabled American explorer William Beebe to become the first person to explore the deep sea.

The bathysphere was a hollow steel ball 4.5 feet (1.4m) in diameter. A solid rubber hose held telephone wires and electricity for lights. A tiny porthole in the side allowed Beebe to observe his surroundings. There was also a 3,500-foot (1,067m) cable that attached the vessel to a barge.

William Beebe (left) and Otis Barton (right) used this bathysphere to explore the deep sea in 1934.

Jacques Piccard

Nearly Seven Miles Down

On January 23, 1960, two men set a world record for deep-ocean exploration. Swiss scientist Jacques Piccard and Donald Walsh of the U.S. Navy descended in a submersible vessel known as *Trieste.* The vessel reached the bottom of the Mariana Trench, which is the deepest point of the ocean. The dive took the explorers nearly 36,000 feet (10,900m) below the surface— a feat of exploration that no one has been able to achieve since.

Prehistory ——

500 B.C. ——

100 B.C. ——

A.D. 100 ——

200 ——

500 ——

1000 ——

1200 ——

1300 ——

1400 ——

1500 ——

1600 ——

1700 ——

1800 ——

1900 ——

2000 ——

2100 ——

After testing the bathysphere for several years, Beebe was ready for his deepest dive. In August 1934, he and his friend, Otis Barton, climbed into the vessel and were lowered into the ocean's inky blackness by the cable. As the men plunged deeper and deeper, Beebe kept up a conversation with his assistant. They had agreed that if he were silent for five minutes, it was a sign he was in trouble.

By the time the expedition was complete, the bathysphere had descended more than 3,000 feet (914m). Beebe observed a strange underwater world that had never been seen by humans, including creatures that no one knew existed. He described his surroundings as a "dark and luminous blue."

Since William Beebe made

The research submarine Trieste *reached a depth of almost seven miles in 1960.*

his historic dive in 1934, many other explorers have followed in his footsteps. Some of them dove five or even ten times deeper than he did. The bathysphere allowed Beebe to be the first person in history to explore the mysterious ocean depths.

Humans in Space

After the deep sea, there remained only one unexplored territory: outer space. For thousands of years scientists and astronomers gazed into the skies and observed the stars and planets. Many dreamed of the day when humans would journey into space. In the 1960s, that dream finally became a reality.

New technology made space exploration possible. Powerful rockets could propel spacecraft hundreds of miles above Earth. Spacesuits protected astronauts and provided them with oxygen when there was little or no air to breathe. Computers plotted the course of spacecraft and guided them on their journeys. Satellite communications equipment allowed astronauts to talk with scientists back on Earth.

Unmanned satellites had been launched in the 1950s, but it was not until 1961 that humans traveled into space. In April of that year, the

Technology in the 1960s made space exploration by rocket possible (left). Above, an American astronaut "walks" in space in 1965.

Prehistory ——

500 B.C. ——

100 B.C. ——

A.D. 100 ——

200 ——

500 ——

1000 ——

1200 ——

1300 ——

1400 ——

1500 ——

1600 ——

1700 ——

1800 ——

1900 ——

2000 ——

2100 ——

Soviet Union made a historical leap in space exploration. Cosmonaut Yuri A. Gagarin became the first person to orbit Earth in a spacecraft. One month later the United States launched its own mission, and astronaut Alan Shepard became the first American in space.

In 1962, astronaut John Glenn became the first American to orbit Earth. The next year, the Soviets launched two spacecraft, one of which carried the first woman into space. The cosmonaut, Valentina Tereshkova, orbited Earth nearly fifty times.

In 1965, Soviet cosmonaut Alexei Leonov became the first human to "walk" in space. That was also a historic year for the United States, because of the Gemini missions, which featured the most advanced spacecraft ever created. The Gemini astronauts used onboard computers to control their own orbits, which had never been done before. They spent a record fourteen days in space, and some of their space walks lasted more than two hours.

For thousands of years, humans were curious about space. Advancements in technology made it possible for them to finally explore it.

The First Space Shuttle

In the 1970s, the United States began building a space shuttle. This spacecraft was different from others because it was designed to be reusable. After a mission, the shuttle would return to Earth and repairs would be made so it could be used on future missions. The first space shuttle was *Columbia*, which launched in 1981. The maiden voyage was successful, and the shuttle was used in many more missions. *Columbia* came to a tragic end in 2003, however. A malfunction caused it to disintegrate as it reentered Earth's atmosphere. All seven astronauts on board were lost.

Astronauts from the Apollo space program were the first people to walk on the Moon.

Men on the Moon

The space missions of the 1960s were the beginning of a new era of exploration. People had been sent into space, and now the Soviet Union and the United States set their sights on the Moon. It would be the greatest challenge ever. The Moon was more than 200,000 miles (321,869km) away. It would take the world's most powerful rocket to send a spacecraft there. When the United States developed the mighty *Saturn V* rocket, a manned Moon mission was possible at last.

On July 16, 1969, the rocket blasted off, propelling the *Apollo 11* spacecraft toward the moon. Four days later, it reached its destination with three astronauts on board: Neil Armstrong, Michael Collins, and Edwin "Buzz" Aldrin. The spacecraft separated, and a lunar module called *Eagle* landed on the Moon's surface. Armstrong and Aldrin were inside *Eagle*, and Collins kept the command module *Columbia* in orbit.

On July 21, Armstrong became the first human to step foot on the Moon. He spoke the famous words: "That's one small step for man, one giant leap for mankind." Aldrin followed shortly thereafter. The astronauts planted an American flag in the lunar soil. They gathered rocks and other materials, performed scientific experiments, and took photographs. A television camera attached to *Eagle* filmed their activities. Two and a half hours later, Armstrong and Aldrin blasted off from the lunar surface in *Eagle*. They docked with *Columbia* and climbed in. Then using its own rocket engines, *Columbia* headed toward Earth. The astronauts arrived safely back home on July 24.

In 1969, for the first time in history, humans explored the Moon. This amazing feat was made possible because of a rocket known as the *Saturn V*, which was powerful enough to send them there.

The Saturn V rocket made the first lunar landing possible.

Wheeling Around the Moon

Apollo 11 was the first of six manned missions to the Moon. The fourth mission, called *Apollo 15*, traveled to the Moon in July 1971. This was different from previous journeys, because the spacecraft carried a small electric car that resembled a dune buggy. The Lunar Roving Vehicle (LRV) weighed almost 500 pounds (227k) on Earth. With almost no gravity on the Moon, it weighed just 80 pounds (36kg) there. After the astronauts landed, they unloaded the little car and drove it around to explore the lunar surface. The LRV traveled about eight miles (0.2k) per hour.

Prehistory —

500 B.C. —

100 B.C. —

A.D. 100 —

200 —

500 —

1000 —

1200 —

1300 —

1400 —

1500 —

1600 —

1700 —

1800 —

1900 —

2000 —

2100 —

The planet Mars

Remote-Control Space Exploration

As exciting as the lunar missions were, scientists dreamed about going far beyond the Moon and exploring deep space. They were especially interested in Mars, because it shared many similarities with Earth. Astronauts could not make the journey, however. Scientists knew there were hazards on Mars that made it too dangerous for humans. In planning the first missions, they designed unmanned spacecraft that could be controlled by people back on Earth.

In 1976, the United States landed *Viking 1* and *Viking 2* on Mars. Scientists wanted the spacecraft to explore different areas, so they programmed them to land thousands of miles apart. As the landers examined the Martian surface, scientists back at mission control gave them instructions and guided their work.

Humans on Mars?

Scientists say a manned Mars mission could occur by 2025. Before that can happen, though, there are hurdles to overcome. For instance, no rocket exists that could make the nearly 300-million-mile (399-million-kilometer) trip to Mars and then travel back to Earth. Astronauts would be inside a spacecraft for about seven months, which would be extremely hard on them. Plus, no spacesuit has been developed that could protect humans against the frigid Martian climate or the planet's suffocating atmosphere. Scientists are working on solving these and many other problems. Until they do, no humans will set foot on the red planet.

This picture from Pathfinder *shows the rocky, dusty surface of Mars.*

Prehistory —

500 B.C. —

100 B.C. —

A.D. 100 —

200 —

500 —

1000 —

1200 —

1300 —

1400 —

1500 —

1600 —

1700 —

1800 —

1900 —

2000 —

2100 —

Twenty years later, the United States launched *Pathfinder*. This spacecraft was unlike any other because it was designed to blast off from Earth and make the rough landing on its own. After speeding through space, *Pathfinder* landed on Mars, bouncing on an enormous cluster of protective airbags. There was also a passenger on the voyage: a tiny roving vehicle named *Sojourner*. Scientists on Earth drove *Sojourner* around the Martian surface by remote control. The rover was fitted with tiny cameras and special equipment to analyze rocks and soil.

In 2003, the United States launched the Mars Exploration Rover (MER) mission, and the two spacecraft landed in 2004. The MER spacecraft each carried a rover: *Spirit* and *Opportunity*. As of fall 2004, the two rovers had explored large areas of the Martian surface. They made some astounding discoveries, such as finding proof that water was once plentiful on Mars.

There are many reasons why it would be valuable for humans to explore Mars. Until that is possible, scientists on Earth will guide and direct spacecraft by remote control.

The United States landed two rovers like this one on the surface of Mars in 2004.

An illustration shows the Cassini *spacecraft orbiting Saturn.* Cassini *has recorded valuable information about the planet's rings.*

A crew readies the Messenger *spacecraft for launch. It should begin orbiting Mercury in 2011.*

Exploration Today

Much has been learned about Mars since the *Viking* missions nearly three decades ago. Yet there are still many more mysteries to be solved. Other Mars missions are planned for the coming years, and they will be launched by the United States as well as other countries.

Exploring other planets is also a priority. For instance, Saturn is being studied by an orbiting spacecraft called *Cassini*. It has taken the temperature of Saturn's rings and found them to be extremely cold—some minus 300°F (149°C). The accompanying *Huygens* probe is examining Titan, Saturn's largest moon.

Also, in August 2004 the United States launched a spacecraft called *Messenger*, whose destination is the planet Mercury. If the mission goes as planned, *Messenger* will begin orbiting Mercury in 2011 and will be the first spacecraft ever to do so. This is exciting because Mercury is the least explored terrestrial, or rocky, planet in the solar system.

In addition to space, modern exploration also focuses on the deep sea. Earth's vast oceans cover nearly three-fourths of the planet's surface, but only a fraction has been explored. Scientists know very little about the deepest parts of the ocean. They want to gain a better understanding of the diverse life that dwells there.

Since ancient times, humans have been curious about the world around them. At first they explored rivers and nearby villages. Over time they crossed vast oceans to explore distant lands. Modern adventurers have explored the deep sea and have ventured into space to unlock the secrets of the solar system. No one knows what tomorrow's exploration will bring, or what discoveries will be made. What is certain is that future explorers will likely possess the same courage, curiosity, and adventurous spirit as the explorers of long ago.

Tropical Mysteries

In addition to space and the ocean, scientists also want to learn more about tropical rain forests. The planet's oldest living ecosystems, rain forests are home to more than half of the world's plant and animal species. Thousands of trees and flowering plants are found in rain forests, as are a wide variety of birds, mammals, reptiles, and butterflies. Also found in rain forests are raw materials used to make life-saving medicines. For instance, rosy periwinkle is found only in the forests of Madagascar. The plant is used to make drugs that treat various forms of cancer.

Mercury is the solar system's least explored rocky planet.

Prehistory ——

500 B.C. ——

100 B.C. ——

A.D. 100 ——

200 ——

500 ——

1000 ——

1200 ——

1300 ——

1400 ——

1500 ——

1600 ——

1700 ——

1800 ——

1900 ——

2000 ——

2100 ——

Glossary

astrolabe: A handheld device used to measure latitude.

bathysphere: The first deep-sea vessel, designed for explorer William Beebe.

cartography: The science of mapmaking.

chip log: An apparatus used to calculate a ship's speed, measured in knots.

chronometer: A precise timekeeping device developed in the nineteenth century.

latitude: A distance north or south of the equator.

longitude: A distance east or west on Earth's surface.

longships: Ships built by Scandinavian explorers known as the Vikings.

magnetite: A mineral with magnetic properties (also called lodestone).

papyrus: An aquatic plant that grows along the banks of rivers.

quadrant: An instrument used to measure latitude.

sextant: An instrument that improved on the astrolabe's ability to measure latitude.

For More Information

Books

William R. Clark, *Explorers of the World.* Garden City, NY: Natural History Press, 1964.

National Geographic Book Service, *Into the Unknown: The Story of Exploration.* Washington, DC: The National Geographic Society, 1987.

Web Sites

BBC Exploration
(www.bbc.co.uk/history/discovery/exploration). An excellent, comprehensive site dedicated to exploration, including a special section for kids.

EOA Scientific
(www.eoascientific.com/cartography). An informative site with valuable information about the science of mapmaking.

National Aeronautics & Space Administration (NASA)
(www.nasa.gov). An outstanding resource with articles, photographs, and a wealth of information about past and current space exploration. Visitors can link to special areas designed just for students.

PBS NOVA Exploration
(www.pbs.org) A very informative site for anyone interested in learning about exploration.

Index